The Archipelago

Owen Hu

BookLeaf Publishing

Presentation by *BookLeaf Publishing*

Web: www.bookleafpub.com

E-mail: info@bookleafpub.com

ISBN: 9789357445481

First edition 2021

DEDICATION

I would like to begin by acknowledging and formally thanking Richard Min for being a mastermind behind The Archipelago. Countless nights of intense work, with hours each session, have translated into the work we have today.

This epic began as an idea. With each successive draft, we saw the characters come to life, the plot more closely resemble the magical realism that we intended, and the world brim with uniqueness. For each successful idea, we threw out ten unsuccessful ones. For each word that made it onto the final manuscript, one thousand words were deleted. For each second that we have worked on The Archipelago, the epic grew closer and closer to what was envisioned. None of this could have been possible without your resolute support, and for that, I am grateful.

Now, we may celebrate how none of our hard work was gone to waste.

ACKNOWLEDGEMENT

To Richard,
An assiduous young man.

PREFACE

The Archipelago is an entirely fantastical world that consists of an infinite number of "islands" in a seemingly endless celestial ocean. Each island is an alternate reality, where the same people and same society live on it, although in slightly different variants. Travel between islands is possible by reaching the coast or recalling once an individual has entered the Interworld ocean already. Millenia Karthas is the central nation-state of each island, and the Inner Circle consists of the ruling Consul's most trusty associates.

Aurora is an ambitious 19-year-old woman who plans on leading Karthas with her political expertise. Jason is a 20-year-old man that grew up with the Fāeryns, a secret religious organization that has historically been persecuted. This story follows their adventures and misfortunes that come with life, a fierce manhunt throughout the archipelago, and the characters' inability to break free of predetermined chains.

Origin

In a fantastical Origin of reverie and vision,
Two characters journey out into the unknown.
From their old homelands they confront division,
Before a disastrous closing trembles their bones.

The great city of Millenia Karthas descends into tumult,
As the secret Fāeryns inaugurate their new commanders.
The people of a glorious millennium rise in revolt,
As a determined new heir is ousted with slanders.

In the archipelago, nothing is secure,
Where a single mistake can spell decisive doom.
Leaders of glamour, of fate, of allure,
Will see the world fall or flourish in full bloom.

Ceremony

Bright rays of sunlight pierced through the crisp waters of the Crystalline,
As the city behind saw the verdant decorations of Millenia Karthas open.
The unwavering sound of a trumpet echoed through the streets between,
As a young woman sits in a coffee shop, brimming with raw emotion.

It is an excellent day to celebrate the birth of Karthas's Great Consuls,
As Aurora Fox enters the doors of the Palace past the stone columns.
A gentle rustle of Karthian harp music sparkles as the red velvet carpet unrolls,
As the festivities saw the Regent give their speeches so solemn.

There were ten political leaders competing to join the Inner Circle,
With Aurora dreaming of this opportunity all her life.
The candidates delivered their remarks as the leaders watched in control,

Before Aurora's speech dazzled the audience
with words like knives.

The consuls arrive back to announce their final
decision,
As Karthas's heir gazes around before his eyes
darken and close.
The lights flicker off as a gun is shot with utmost
precision,
As a sickening thump sounds the fall of the
Consul's bodies once so grandiose.

Chaos isn't when the hearts of the people are
torn into a million pieces,
But rather when the people are united under a
single extreme thought.
A thousand terrified souls scream through the
halls as confusion increases,
As the Karthian heir vengefully vows the
assassin will be caught.

Homeland

Chiming bells strike, signaling a desolate midnight,
As a young man finds peace in a sacred network of caves.
At last he emerges in an expansive dome of incandescent light,
As he follows the secret Priests in the paths they pave.

The Fāeryn faith sees the Quintus stand atop the waterfall,
As they announce the challenge to find the Fāeryns' true home.
Jason Aurum accepts the quest when leaving the cave walls,
In the barren wastelands of the Origin he begins to roam.

The rugged peaks of Mount Origin loom in the distance behind,
As Jason scales the ranges of the pinnacling spired mountains.
Scorching heat dampens his search before the stars align,

As he loses his quest in seeking the homeland
fountain.

On the last day of the challenge nothing is new,
Until he unravels the wilderness and hears a
thundering roar.
The Fāeryn homeland lays ahead in full view,
As Jason exhaustedly slumps onto the dirt and
gravel floor.

The charming village of the Skyfall is the home
of the Fāeryns,
Hidden by towering trees and a waterfall that
cascades the sky.
Brilliantly ornamented hardwood buildings buzz
with men,
As the highlands welcome the fifth arrival with a
rejoicing cry.

Chaos

Aurora gazes out the palace windows after the mayhem,
Seeing a city under lockdown, of sirens wailing in the air.
The heir on the balcony addresses the assassins he so condemns,
Before he turns to Aurora, a cold gaze with eyes so fair.

An accusation of malicious murder is spoken as all eyes turn to her,
So Aurora backs in confusion before the Karthian Guards arrive.
She had no idea who the assassin was or where they were,
But that is no deterrent to the heir as out the window Aurora dives.

Running through the desolate streets of a city once so magnificent,
Aurora desperately escapes from the pandemonium and confusion.
She knew she was not the killer but could not prove her innocence,

As she roars away in her car believing the
situation to be an illusion.

The shouting of the pursuing Guards are left
behind,
As Aurora escapes her home and out to the city
limits.
There was no time to rejuvenate, no time to find
her peace of mind,
How had her perfect life changed in just a single
minute?

Fleeing Karthas in a mix of rage, panic, and
bitterness,
She could not help but feel sorrowful for the life
she has abandoned.
Her hopes and dreams mirrored the unbounded
wilderness,
As Aurora sought safety in Mount Origin's
rugged command.

Inauguration

An introduction to the other four recruits is followed by relief,
As Jason learns of the true motive behind the Quintus' quest.
They will be training to lead the Fāeryn, to be the next chiefs,
To pass down a secret of the Origin that has their civilization possessed.

The days fly by in the sacred little hollow,
As the blackbirds take flight from the Skyfall mist.
The five recruits are each assigned a Quintus to follow,
As scripts are memorized and the Fāeryn ways persist.

With the long days of religious training now behind the recruits,
The inauguration ceremony will formally take place.
At the summit of Mount Origin they are tested by their faithful roots,
As each is called on to vow a statement of grace.

A female recruit known as Callie stands out as her name is called,
Retrieving a knife before aiming it at the leading Quintus's head.
Two other Quintus suffer the same fate as the crowd looks appalled,
As the distressed recruits call for aid for the murderous bloodshed.

The stabbing on Mount Origin leaves no one free,
As the remote summit hears a thousand petrified wails.
Jason scrambles down the slopes in an attempt to flee,
Forcing down logic and allowing his emotions to prevail.

Golden Meadows

At the base of Mount Origin Aurora collapses in fatigue,
Before rocks tumble down in a tumultuous flash.
Raising her head, she perceives a white-robed man of intrigue,
As he halts to a stop from his summit-to-base dash.

The man introduces himself as Jason, on an escape from turmoil,
As Aurora remains skeptical of man's true intentions.
She wearily trusts Jason to not have her getaway plans be foiled,
And they devise a breakout plan without further intervention.

They travel on the road leading out of civilization,
Unsure of what to expect in the paths they take.
Outside the modern cityscapes are towns of isolation,
Before the dirt road leads to hamlets down by a lake.

Several days into their travels they stop by an idyllic meadow,
With emerald blades of grass transformed golden by the setting sun.
The faraway treelines are hued with a dazzling glow,
Where the flowers rustle, the creek flows, and the worries are none.

As their frantic getaway draws to a peaceful end,
The initial moods of panic are replaced with joy.
The zephyrs of late-summer breezes accompany the friends,
When the Guards catch up with the intent to destroy.

The Interworld

Aurora and Jason are on the edges of a jagged cliff,
With still ocean waters as far as the eye can see.
The shouts of the Guards in a manner so stiff,
Creates no chance of an escape for the two to be.

With no other direction other than down the cliffs of immense height,
The pair embrace each other in trust before leaping off together.
In the fall from the top, keeping calm takes immense might,
Before the pair silently splashes into the serene seas, light as a feather.

The world ripples in a magical veil of shimmers,
As disorientation takes hold of any previous impressions.
A distant light begins to shine a minuscule glimmer,
As the pair arrive in the Interworld, a confusing mix of expressions.

An endless sea of islands each glow a distinct white,

As the pair's consciousnesses drift between the lands.
With an infinite copy of the same world in flight,
The alternate dimensions ahead may meet all demands.

Each Origin is simply a microscopic point on a grid,
None unique, with infinite copies of the same world.
The Interworld allows for travels with nothing to be hid,
Between the dimensions where the secret is not hurled.

Aura

As Aurora drifts through the islands of mystery,
She considers the possibilities of each one.
Each world is the same, with matching histories,
Yet each world holds prospects of hopes just begun.

How she had come to this mystifying position remains a question,
Her encounter with Jason had to be something greater than fate.
All she wanted was to join the Inner Circle to lead Karthas with suggestions,
Now she found herself hiding in the unknown in a miserable state.

Who was the black-hearted assassin to have spawned all her troubles,
To have been the one to ruin her one opportunity at achieving anything good?
Why had the heir betrayed her when she was certain of joining the Circle's double,
When she had no involvement in the assassination, where she was misunderstood?

Shaking herself back to the present,

Aurora felt Jason tugging her near.
There was an aura of something pleasant,
An intrigue in one of the islands ever so clear.

So the pair drifted together towards the light,
Unsure of how to leave this state of limbo.
Nearer and nearer towards the island of white,
The world shimmered again like a time long ago.

Failure

Jason was back in his body above the clouds,
Insecure over his predicament of where he had appeared.
Only when he recognized the ceremony and the crowds,
Did a sense of dread of his past life begin to take fear.

Back atop Mount Origin processing the ceremony,
The Quintus called the recruits one by one.
When Callie was called, Jason called her a phoney,
In an effort to have the disaster in this world be undone.

Callie pulls out her knife and aims it at Jason,
Who is prepared and dodges the deadly throw.
With future perceptions of otherworldly information,
He warns everyone else before going for a blow.

The Quintus are still too slow as Callie takes aim,
Their blood soaking the barren soil ground.

How had Jason failed to prevent such pain,
Was an answer he could not come around.

His failure recalled him to his parents of old,
Who had disappeared and abandoned him as a child.
The Fāeryns were generous enough to foster him bold,
But being a failure again was not something worth a smile.

Ecstasy

Aurora finds herself in an alternate world of peace,
A world where the heir that she loved never betrayed her.
There was nothing to complain about, no worries to release,
She was happier in this reality than she and Jason ever were.

She enjoyed lazy afternoons of floating in the Palace pools with the heir,
And enjoys luxurious dinner feasts at each royal banquet.
Being a part of the Inner Circle, she had not a single tear,
There was nothing other than happiness in this world as of yet.

Aurora gave royal speeches full of vigour and passion,
Representing one of Karthas's ten districts was a dream come true.
Her new life of euphoric ecstasy had fulfilled her ambition,

Even with the pain of her past life, she had still
pulled through.

It was another evening of pleasure with the heir,
her lover,
When the late-autumn breeze ruffled her hair as
they sat on the Palace rooftop.
Even in her joy, there was still so much more to
discover,
As she enjoyed the flickering city lights when a
sound made her heart stop.

The unmistakable sound of an explosion
violently burst through the calm night sky,
As the heir dashed back into the Palace to
determine what was wrong.
Aurora followed, with golden chandeliers
lighting up the bodies of the Consuls that had
died,
And, for the first time in forever, Aurora wept
and did not feel so strong.

The Archipelago

Just like how his parents had forsaken him,
Jason abandoned the others,
Running away from his failure to prevent the killings.
He was flushed with shame at having acted like his father and mother,
But now was not the time to grieve his misgivings.

He willed to leave this wretched world behind,
But the coastal cliffs were too far out to travel to.
Promising this mountain would not be a place to be confined,
Jason firmly imagined the Interworld that he knew.

His consciousness left his body as his mind drifted away,
The shimmering once again accompanying his entry into the zone.
He would not give in to his failures and to his dismay,
He found himself in the archipelago of the unknown.

A concoction of emotions seemed to overwhelm his wits,
As Jason drifted along the dark sea through the infinite islands of light.
He longed for company, but each world was too much to commit,
And his consciousness failed to move as he sensed something was not right.

Jason was lost in the Interworld archipelago,
A lone soul with no homeland to return to.
He would endlessly fall to the lowest of the low,
In search of a life that could not be true.

Ruination

The heir had turned bitter once again as if possessed,
As Aurora let loose an inferno of pure rage.
The villains of the previous world had caught up to her rest,
And she found herself completely helpless to engage.

A marble pillar crashed as Aurora punched it with all her might,
Vexed at this cruel world for ripping away the only happiness she had ever known.
She gallantly flipped an ornament table with all of her ill spite,
Indignant at the world for forcing her to flee from Karthas again, all alone.

The Guards began flooding through the halls,
A reminder for Aurora to leave this ruined place.
She heard the Guards shout ferocious calls,
But Aurora burst out the Palace and kept her pace.

She suddenly stopped running, considering an acceptance of her destiny:

If she would be caught and executed, so be it.
Even if she lost her liberty, her mind would be free,
But she snapped out and did not let them catch up one bit.

Unable to outrun the Guards forever,
Aurora attempted to travel to another universe.
She let her mind drift with a great endeavour,
But the Guards cornered her like a curse.

Ascension

After aimlessly drifting for what feels like an
eternity,
A deep voice echoes across the dark seas.
Jason is unsure whether he hears it internally or
externally,
But the voice compels him to smile in glee.

The voice explains that he is in ascension,
A state of both loneliness and power.
He patrols the Interworld in attention,
In search of lost souls to empower.

Jason pleas to be placed in the world where
Aurora is,
But he is responded to with a sound of regret.
To deal with Aurora's situation is a role that is
not his,
But Jason insists on finding Aurora, with a hint
of a threat.

At last the voice gives in,
Warning the reflective Jason to be careful.
The shimmering begins again,
As an understanding Jason emerges in the world
dareful.

He sees the same golden-eyed Aurora as before,
But now she is in torn clothes and cornered by Karthian Guards.
Aurora lets out a weep that shakes Jason's core,
So Jason crashes through the Guards, watching them fall like a deck of cards.

The Map

The Guards stop as Jason cowers beside Aurora,
As she looks him in the eye with confusion and shock.
Aurora feels Jason radiate a distinct, determined aura,
As the Guards taunt the two in a laughing mock.

Jason wraps his arms around Aurora's shoulders,
As Aurora maintains her intense gaze on her chasers.
As the Guards closed in, Aurora prepares to lob a boulder,
But Jason stops Aurora and tightly embraces her.

In the moment before the Guards reach the pair,
A shimmering darkness envelopes Aurora's mind.
Anticipating traveling to another world of despair,
She instead finds herself with the Interworld in bind.

Unlike her previous travels throughout the mysterious realm,

Aurora now sees the entire map of the world
panned below.
Jason informs her that they are in ascension and
to not be overwhelmed,
As the grid-like map of the archipelago of
islands glows.

Despite feeling relief, Aurora couldn't help but
regret her choice,
Her choice to continue on living a life that will
never again peak in happiness.
As she contemplates her indecisions Aurora
discerns a voice,
And her state of ascension makes her small and
insignificant life feel meaningless.

Unity

The voice had taught Jason how to ascend at command,
And he had passed on this knowledge to help Aurora out.
In that moment of fear, they were together hand in hand,
But Jason was sure that they would escape and had no doubts.

Now high above the lightless seas,
The archipelago of islands seems so small.
The emotion that had overtaken him had finally eased,
As the grid formation below started to call.

The light islands were in perfect unity,
None wavering, all shining ever so bright.
It seemed as if Jason had lost all opportunity,
When an island began flickering into the night.

Jason's consciousness sensed the light begin to dim,
As the undisturbed seas cradled the light in support.

Sensing Aurora's mutual understanding with him,
He let himself fall into the still ocean of sorts.

The dark seas were not cold as he expected,
But he and Aurora swam towards the dimming island.
Towards a new world of hope, he directed,
Before the pair finally made it out onto the dryland.

Disarray

As a veil of distortion enveloped her vision,
Aurora found herself standing by the Crystalline.
She was in a Karthas of disarray and division,
Where the banners were not emerald but instead a dull green.

With Jason beside her, Aurora bit her tongue as she glanced around,
Fires were burning, and dust and smoke blew through the air as a building collapsed.
The Consuls had been assassinated, and the new heir was being crowned,
As citizens swarmed the streets of a nation whose time had finally elapsed.

More refugees crowded out of once-modern institutions,
As loudspeakers announced a recent declaration of war.
Millennia Karthas was in a state of civil revolution,
Where a clamorous mob of anarchy cannot resist anymore.

Aurora grabs Jason's arm as the pair hurry along the Crystalline perimeter,
Unsure of what to do, unsure of where to go to escape this uproar.
Karthas, a kingdom in its golden age, had lost its glory to those who were bitter,
Now it was unclear what would become of this world now ignored.

An explosion sounded in the distance as the chants of the mob grew louder,
With Aurora stuck in her path of senseless escape under the early-winter sun.
The Karthas that she knew—the place that she could call home—could not make her prouder,
But in this Origin, nothing could redeem this kingdom that is damned and done.

Shattered

Jason knew that the Crystalline, like the coast, was an escape to an alternate dimension,
But was unsure of what would occur if too many people used it at once.
Halting Aurora's desperate run, he looks her in the eye as he called for attention,
As he knew that Karthas was crumbling simultaneously on many fronts.

If they were to stay in this Origin any minute longer than they need to,
They would be endangering their lives as the revolution escalates.
After much careful consideration and much intense review,
Jason informs Aurora of the Crystalline as a way to separate.

It was very much a mistake to travel to this reality,
And an escape was urgent as the explosions continued.
Suddenly the colours of the world unsaturated in abnormality,

As the world dimmed into darkness and the wind blew.

The world intensified as the contrast increases,
With horrified screams replacing the chants.
Fragments of reality began to shatter into pieces,
As citizens collapsed as if in a trance.

The world finally blacked out as Jason saw a glimpse,
Of the Interworld showing through the cracked abyss.
He was unable to move, feeling his whole body limp,
As he had his thoughts run his life reminisce.

The Last Frontier

Aurora witnessed the scene with horror,
As Jason goes limp and slumps onto the ground.
A great nation now in a state of disorder,
Aurora must leave before to death she is bound.

Abandoning Jason's unmoving body on the
concrete,
She runs to the Crystalline railings and stands on
the ledge.
She would never allow herself to die in
undignified defeat,
And at the final crack of an explosion she leaps
off the edge.

In the Interworld she commands her mind to go
into ascension,
And Aurora soars above the archipelago to the
top.
She glances down at the grid-like map with
much apprehension,
Before she sees a scene that makes her heart
stop.

The grid flashes and trembles with tremendous force,
As the surrounding islands feel a shockwave.
Aurora laments the people of the world with remorse,
Before reminding herself that they could not be saved.

At long last the world is claimed by the ocean,
As the shine dims to darkness and the lights disappear.
Her consciousness dulls in her unfolding devotion,
As the island is devoured by the everlasting frontier.

Fate

Jason awakes from his faintness and rises from his stance,
As he sees an anguished Aurora balancing on the rails.
More chaos unfolds as the world shatters and the colours dance,
But Jason does not bother warning her as he knows he will fail.

The Crystalline was constructed by the Fāeryns as a one-way portal,
Where under any ordinary circumstance entering the water would bring no effect.
Only in an extreme situation would those who jump become immortal,
Forever trapped in the Interworld as a way for the souls to live on unchecked.

A massive tremble shocks the city,
As Karthas is brought to its very knees.
When Aurora jumps, Jason feels only pity,
As Karthas is ruined by the disease of greed.

More shockwaves reverberate around the region,
And the light flickers as Aurora makes a splash.

Without any thought, Jason runs and gives a
reason,
As buildings crumble and disintegrate into ash.

The final parts of the world begin to shatter,
As he takes a leap of faith into the water.
Whether Jason arrives in time does not matter,
As he would only be one of many that were
slaughtered.

Eternal

After the point on the grid is vanquished,
Aurora watches in unmoving disbelief.
She feels herself begin to languish,
But strangely notices a lack of grief.

A new light replaces the old,
As the grid is complete once again.
A sense of understanding takes hold,
As she rests into a state of zen.

Aurora contemplates her new life,
Reflecting on the actions she had done.
She comprehends no internal strife,
Her mind and thoughts finally one.

Enough reflection later,
Aurora drifts down.
There is something greater,
That she must navigate around.

But trying her previous method of leaving the
Interworld yielded no results,

As it dawns on Aurora that she is unable to leave this dark ocean.
With no one around to keep her company, no one around for her to consult,
She acknowledges that the archipelago is her new home, her perpetual motion.

Darkness

The marching of time slows in the seconds after Jason jumps, but darkness envelopes him. A golden aurora blazing across the midnight darkness is the final thing he sees before all goes black.

www.ingramcontent.com/pod-product-compliance
Lightning Source LLC
Chambersburg PA
CBHW051742130826
49812CB00033B/974

* 9 7 8 9 3 5 7 4 4 5 4 8 1 *